TEEN
ACHE

SHREYAS SUSAN VARGHESE

TEEN ACHE

PARTRIDGE
A Penguin Random House Company

To order additional copies of this book, contact
Partridge India
000 800 10062 62
orders.india@partridgepublishing.com

www.partridgepublishing.com/india

Contents

THE LITTLE DEVIL IN ME

I may look sweet and demure
But never judge anyone by their looks
cause there's a little devil in me
that sprouts up time and again

When I wish my friend good luck for the exam

In my mind I make a quickie
silent prayer
that she should flunk...
When we dress up for a party
I do not bother to tell her that
she looks like a guppy fish
I think that's for others to say

When I visit a home
I compliment the plump hostess
on her figure
When my best friend's out of
earshot
I tell everyone at listening
length what a mean girl she is...

I make sure that I give alms in
public
watched by atleast four people
I make sure that I give a tip
only
when in company

I blissfully forget to recharge
my mobile
when I am the sole possessor of
a mobile in my gang
I feign to be in the bathroom
when mom calls me for a job
I make sure that the priest
sees me
regularly praying in the church

And I always make sure that no
one sees
the little devil in me
and I am sweet and demure
to all...

Tears –the magical liquid

Every morning putting my contact lens on,
I prick my eyes and there it comes
Pouring like the uninvited early monsoon
Coursing its path through my face powder caked face
A betrayal to my original colour

I am falsely accused
When I haven't done anything
Anger flares up
I ruffle like an angry hen
Ready to peck
My voice quivers and shivers
My opponents start crucifying me
And there comes an uninvited
enemy
Wetting my cheeks
Betraying the fact that I really
was a wimp
My opponents console me, pat
me on my back
I move out miserable as ever

My bestie got elected as school
president
And I lose it big time
I pretend to be happy for her
But in the inside I was shattered
Devastated to be precise
My friend hugs me in ecstasy
Two little drops wet her shoulder
A brutal betrayal to the
Real envious little creature I am

My boyfriend ditches me and I
suffer a heart break
I tell him that I was anyways
going to ditch him
I pretend a false laugh, a cool
smirk

But like the great Bengal flood
Tears gush down my eyes, nose
and cheeks
He hugs me, consoling me
that I would get a better guy
Betrayal to the fact that I loved
him like hell

I go to my aunt's funeral
Dressed in black
As funeral ready as I could be
All cousins, aunts and uncles,
stuff wads of tissues
In their eyes, nose and where not

My eyes are like the Sahara
desert
Not even a single tear
I panic try to think of all the
terrible
Incidents in my life
But alas not even a single drop
Tears you betrayed me, brutal
betrayal...

What is one minute to you??.

For me it's the time to bubble an MCQ
For me it's that one minute which determines
My dreams and aspirations
For an actress one minute is the time to be herself
When she is no longer, wife of somebody
or lover of another...

For a thug it's the time to choose
which house to rob
For a sportsman it's the key to
recognition and fame

For a toddler it's the time to
gasp for breath
before bawling again
For a dying man it's the time to
express and expose who he
really was

Sixty seconds can change
anyone's life
A murderer can drop his knife and
become saintly
A prostitute may feel a guilt
pang
and turn back
Your little heart can beat
seventy two times
You can breathe sixteen times
You can forgive someone and
forget someone
You can change the course of
your life
in just sixty seconds...

Pain, pads and pallor...
PERIODS... again!!!

A monthly dilemma
For every XX chromosome
Not sure whether boon or bane
But unanimously unwelcome to all
A dilemma that's PERIODS!!!

In my younger days
I was terrified at the
Prospect, afraid whether I would
Die bleeding...

Teachers, parents and siblings
All explaining in their own ways
What it was all about
But none too clear, none too
precise

They told this and that
Touching neither here nor there
But I was sure some interesting
facts were left out
Set an adolescent mind to ponder
And you are asking for trouble

School libraries found a new
purpose
In internet I discovered a new
teacher
And similar ones of my age
All brought in new theories

Sanitary pads always attracted
me
Felt envious when adults took
two or three
Different coloured packets

I enter into my teens and there
One day I am greeted with
A stomach pain
Which I later learnt was
mittelschmerz

Menarche was no fun
Those sanitary pads were
nothing marvelous
From menarche I was on
constant vigil
For periods which docked
between dates
Never on the right time

It came on my sports day, my school day
The days I chose to wear white
The days I planned to go swimming
And along with it came mood swings and depression
An outburst of angry red pimples

I still curse the day that I longed for sanitary pads!!

Jeans

Her waist size is 32
But she screams for a
size 28
I don't know why she is persisting
And she takes me down from
The pretty mannequin who had
me on,
I go with her, reluctant
Poor 28 sized blue denim I was
after all . . .

At her home she forces me on
I feel gagged, suffocated
After an hour's ordeal
She is wearing me
She flaunts me in her friends'
circles
She wipes sticky hands on me
My pockets become a mini mobile
beauty salon

When she's back home
She seeks her mom's help to
remove me
I wail at the cruel treatment
bestowed
But who is to listen to poor
jeans?

After a year I wonder
Why I am never washed
Then I understand the trend
The dirtier, the trendier

I get scratched and bruised
When she jumps hostel walls
After late night parties
But no one listens to me

Some days I would be too tired
Still she would wear me
I guess I was too good
To be worn out in all occasions

I panic whether I would get
asthma attacks
I am clogged with dust, dirty
wads of chewing gum
And my pockets are crammed
with
Stolen pocket money and an
Assortment of lip balms
And her irritating mobile
Which bangs out like a fire alarm
Every other second . . .

I long to go back to my peaceful
life
Hanging lazily on a shop window
Waited on hand and foot by
pretty salesgirls
In the big mall
Envious girls eyeing me
Ahh that was life . . .

THE MYSTERY
ABOUT GOD...

From my childhood days
   I have been thrust upon
this idea
of God watching whatever I do
His eyes never missing a thing

I swallowed this whole heartedly
When I became a little big

I wondered why God didn't tell
my mom
when I sneaked and stayed till
midnight

And then I understood that God
was
not a stringent cop as I thought
And then it became a habit of
calling
God's name before a little pick
pocketing from my dad's pocket

Or like praying to God to not let
me be caught
in the film theatre bunking
classess...

In my teenage days
the lover who didn't care,the
friend who betrayed,
parents who didn't bother all
became debatable issues with
God
I cried and bawled at God for
my lost love,friendship and a lot
more...

From then on I was a chameleon
travailing through being agnostic
when something was going to go
bad
atheistic when it had already
gone bad
and pious as ever when some
little
surprises I never expected
became true...

But still even in my atheistic
phase
I know that he's just a call away
He knows my tantrums,drama
emotions everything

He's my love and career guru
my emotional manager
my   heavenly   beautician,my
personal stylist

Now I am in my atheistic phase
but still I can't help myself but
pray in my subconscious mind
Oh God let this poem be good
enough!!!!...

THE URGE TO PEE

It has constantly bothered me in my conscious mind whenever I am out of my home I have an urgent need to pee...

Advices came from many sides and I took the most logical one avoid all fluid intakes once out of home

So here I am in my dad's
colleague's home
out for supper
The hostess comes with coffee
for all

I politely refuse saying I do not
like hot beverages
She leaves, I am relieved
But the relief whooshes out of
me
As soon as I see her returning
with a giant glass of lemonade

I couldn't be impolite
I drink the lemonade hoping
that at least the supper would
be solid

But where's luck
I am met with an assortment of
soups
I rush through the main courses
and as I laugh at my father's
jokes
my epiglottis forces open

And there I am gasping...
people thumping me on the head
and again glasses of water
drained into my throat
I had learnt that micturition is
a voluntary process
and I silently prayed it would
remain so...

And then again comes the host
with a tag line of
we will talk over drinks
Dirty old man
I felt like peeing on his Persian
carpet

After what seemed like a
fortnight
we reached our home
I make a beeline for the
bathroom
the familiar smell of harpic
greeting me

The white closet
never had I been this happy
as my urethra contracts and
my bladder lets go...

Nirbhaya

After my death
I was christened Nirbhaya
One who doesn't fear
But you don't know the real
story
Or the fear that lurched me
each second
Whenever I saw their lustful
Beady eyes asking for more
wanting more. . .

After a wonderful movie
With my friend
We made our way
Through the familiar streets of
Delhi
Our minds in sync with the Delhi
traffic
Which was like a lullaby to us

And then came a vehicle
Like a death chariot I later
realized
Slowly stealthily through the
Delhi roads
The vehicle that devoured my
chastity
Which made me wish for death
Rather than being tortured alive

We waved our hands, and the
bus stopped
We felt excited, happy
Never did I know that
It was the last bus I would catch
in my life
The last smile in my life as
I climbed the steps to hell

Once inside, some men watched
me
It was uncomfortable, trust me
Like a hawk eyeing a prey
They eyed me
Panic developed in me
I caught my friend's hand
For assurance, and he comforted
me

I revisited some lessons of positive thinking
I imagined myself to be back in my home
Narrating the story of how I was nearly in trouble
I mentally laughed, imagining the panic attack it would cause to my parents
How they would tell a quick prayer
And how they would hug me
Glad that I was back home . . .

But sometimes imaginations do not
Develop into realities
And sadly for me, this one didn't
Within some seconds, the whole atmosphere changed
My friend was beaten and thrown out of the bus
I couldn't do anything . . .

The only one time that I regretted
About being a girl was that moment
But the woman in me resurfaced
I had read in an old book that
One could smell death
And I smelt it, the smell of cruel torturous death

Quotes echoed through my mind
Cowards die many times
But the valiant taste of death
only once
So this was my time
And I would die a warrior

I fought with all my might
Never letting myself give up
I pictured my parents in my
mind
Thinking they would be proud
of me
That I fought like a warrior

They devoured me, tore me apart
But physical blows meant nothing to me
In my mind, I built a wall of steel
I fought as a woman, a proud woman . . .

Among those lustful animals
There was even a guy who could
Have been my younger brother
Some the age of my dad
I didn't let anything of this dishearten me

That day I understood how much an
Indian woman could do
And now I understood why India gave birth to
Warriors like Jhansi Rani

Death was my reward, but who cares
Still I remain alive in all your minds
When you light candles for me
And christen me as Nirbhaya . . .

I am comforted, my bruises healed
Fight, sisters, fight
Be a proud Indian woman
Nothing to fear . . . fight . . .
Nirbhaya

Never turn back
you can't

I wish I was still that
Toddler,   with   a   milk
moustache
And small helpless flailing arms
Who could be hushed by a milk
bottle?

Or   those   innocent   primary
school days
When any of my tantrums could
be

Tackled by a box of chocolates
And there I would forget
everything
And run to my mother

Those high school days
And I was in cloud nine
The excitement of being a teen
An assortment of hormones
coursing through my veins
I waged wars for talk offers,
net recharges
And a rise in pocket money

Come college days and I
withdrew to my new world
I craved to go for parties,
hangout with friends
Deny me the permission and you
see the devil in me

I started throwing tantrums
No longer can anyone comfort me
My mom watches me concerned
As I crouch in the loneliness of
my room
Lost in a world where no one can
reach out to me

Deep inside I am still that little
girl
Who could be pacified by that
milk bottle?
But to the world I am a troubled
headstrong teenager
Who is in the world of cyber
addiction...
Who is betrayed by her love...
Who is cheated by her friends...
Whose exams give her the
nightmares...

Her odd ways...
Her guilty conscience...
Her confused mind...

Battling between morals and temptations
      Friends and parents...
      Dreams and realities...
She is confused, unable to decide
Unable to push herself
She prefers to cuddle back into her mom's lap
Forgetting all her troubles
But she is unable to
Because she is no longer that small child
Pacified by that milk bottle

To the world she is an eighteen
plus individual
With her own likes and dislikes
No one else can forgive her
She hides behind an anonymity
cloak
Withdraws more and more into
the core of problems

Help comes from no one
Help comes from no where
She tries to change
But the world is too harsh to
accept changes
You can never be that little girl
again

You have grown through the
years
Lost your innocence
Your sweet and demure
expression
Your guilt is your cross
You can never change back
So, proceed with life
Putting on a mask
A mask of fake boldness
A mask of I don't care attitude
And face the world
Because innocence is something
you can never buy back...

Pediculosis

An uninvited enemy enters
into a territory
Without your consent
Without your knowledge
Grazes away in that pasture of
Conditioner fed, protein nourished,
spa treated forest...sipping your
blood

Making you conscious
Those itchy crawly LICE!!
Maybe from a packed bus or
Your less neat friend who
Grabs you for a selfie

They invade you anytime
anywhere
Those silky straight locks,
No longer seem so pretty
In the class you sit perfect
Feeling itchy but all you do is
poke your
Pen on your scalp
Putting on an intelligent
expression

You stick to dark coloured
dresses for a while
You go to far away medical shops
To buy anti-lice creams and
shampoos
Making a quick getaway
You can't scratch when you want to
All you do is show a gesture
Pretending to smoothen your
tresses
To pacify that itch
And devise new plans to get rid of
Those creepy crawly parasites.....

Pride goes before a fall

When you see me,
  You are sure not to miss,
Those dark kohl lined eyes,
Sheltered under arched eyebrows

Plunge and you will see their
depth...
My pride my beauty
I emoted with my eyes and I did
overdo it
flaunted them for selfies

And fluttered my mascara clad eyelids
The overall effect was awesome!!!

Pride goes before a fall.
So have I heard and so did I ruminate
When I sat in the optical awaiting my turn
Astigmatism combined with myopia
I call this quite a Christmas gift
I go back looking like a grandma from folklore

I am met with smirking glances
and suppressed laughter
On my maiden visit to class with
my specs
Nerds swarm around me
May be happy at the prospect
of a new member to their crew

I feel hopeless when I see my
face in a mirror
I feel my beautiful eyes are
dead
Buried in sockets and the specs
serve as the coffin lids
Burying their beauty...

Never let me know
it was you

Slap me in the face
Hit me hard
I can take all that
But never a sly dig
Never do I want to know that
you were
Behind trapping me
You used my innocence, misused
my trust

A request to you
Cheat me but never let me know
that
Your caring eyes could ever do
that
Your lips that spoke sweet words
Forced me into a maze that
I can never escape from...

Slap me, but slap me in the face
But make sure that my eyes are
closed
Because it hurts me more not
when I am
Cheated but when I know that
it was
You who cheated me...

Say cheese!!!!

I hate the visit to the studio
To sit in uncomfortable whacky chairs
Even eyelids intact
Pasting fake smiles

How can a photographer ask me to smile?
Does he know that I came here after a funeral??

The ordeal of taking it again
and again
He says "shoulders up and ah
now slightly right
Tilt your chin
There you are now look at me..."

After seeing him, the way even
in my
lips twitched to a dry smile
Drew itself into a straight line
After all these trying times
And seeing my print of the photo
Looking like a frog in the
moonlight
I wonder whether it was worth
all the trouble...

Confessions of a Royal Bengal Tiger

This is based on a true incident which happened in a zoo in Delhi.

It was a hot afternoon
And I was lazy
Mighty bored to be precise
Many jobless people clicking
Pictures of me
Children breaking their necks
to see my
Majestic appearance

I roar majestically
Just to show them the power
of a
Royal Bengal tiger
They crane their necks and look
at me
With greedy little eyes

But I am fed up; I ignore them
and think of
My lush green jungle and
The cool water of the stream
My hunting games and much
more . . .
And then I pass into a short
slumber

And I am rudely awoken by some
Irritating camera flashes
Directly into my eyes
I growl and wake up displeased to
Be woken up from my peaceful
dreams of
Lush green forests

I wake up and find myself in the
silly enclosure
And a swarm of greedy-eyed
humans outside . . .
And then I see a fragile figure
Crouched in the corner of my
enclosure, my territory
The territory of the Royal
Bengal tiger . . .

I ignore him
Too bored to even react
And then the greedy swarm of
monsters
Started pelting me with stones,
paper, and whatnot . . .
I shake myself

No longer do I see the scared
figure
Crouching in my territory as a
fragile creature
I see him as a greedy human

Who snatched away my lush
green home
Who kept me caged
Snatched my freedom
Who made the Bengal tiger
A clown to be photographed, to
be guffawed at . . .
I saw him as the representative
of that greedy lot of humans

I growled and walked towards him
The execution of death penalty
Clearly in my mind
But when I reached near him
Compassion stole over me
He was a human skeleton
Skin and bones
He was nothing in front of me

But then I saw his pleading hands
His eyes pleaded for death . . .
Begged for mercy
I was stunned
Unable to decide

And then I understood that
death was
A safer heaven for that skin
and bones
Rather than the cruel world
outside
Our eyes locked for a second
And I realized our stories were
similar
For me, my cage was a prison
And for him, his life was a prison

Hunger, poverty, and misery battled in his
Sunken eyes
And I heard his prayer and as
Gently as I could, I gave him a final pat
The pat that pushed him to heaven
Away from the cruel onlookers
Still flashing their greedy cameras
Happy about the show the
Royal Bengal tiger had put forth

I turned my back, ignored them
Walked majestically, happy
That I had done something good
in my life
The life of a
Royal Bengal tiger.

ME-THE ESCAPIST

The escapist in me looks down
When a teacher scans the rows
For a doubtful face to charge
her question

The escapist in me sleeps off
When I flunk an exam
It never thinks about tomorrow
Never thinks about next hour

The escapist in me shies away
When I am the first to enter
Into an unknown host's home

The escapist in me catches an
imaginary cold
When my exam portions are out
of control
The escapist in me should escape
from me lest
I become a wimpy person

But here again the escapist in me
shuffles away at the prospect
of escaping from me
So here it's back again!!!

Where is freedom??

When I am born
I am tied to my mother
with the umbilical cord
When the nurse cuts it
I wail, maybe happy at the
prospect of freedom

Little do I realize that I am
taken to
A cage with bars...a little crib
I bawl having found that I have lost
My newly found freedom

From nursery to school
All my movements watched by
Hawk eyed teachers

Questioning   parents   at
doorsteps
When I am five minutes late
Checking call registers
Accessing my facebook account
I feel caged...

After my marriage I think
At last FREEDOM
Again I see that I am always
questioned
All my movements watched
In-laws add to my stalkers list

When my children grow up in
My old age I am met by
questioning eyes
Whenever I grope for an extra
fruit
When age grows
I am parented by them too

In my death my freedom is still
curbed
Me who is claustrophobic
Kept in a closed dark coffin...

A tarnished face ...
an unscathed soul

You might have seen me in
a crowded bus
Sitting alone at the aisle seat
Or in the busy roads
All alone none to walk beside me

You are sure not to miss me,
Probably even talked about me
Though never to me...
The lady with the half eaten face
Or the lady with the ugly scar

These are some I have heard
myself
When you people don't bother
to hush your tones
I don't know what you would
have called me
Had you seen me

I was good at chemistry maybe
even brilliant
I loved those chemicals all
bottled up
Fizzing and fuming in the closed
constraints

The fumes of nitric acid...
The golden yellow of sulphur
The blue vibrant copper sulphate
Reminding me of the ocean
bottled up in a glass can

But trust me I never knew that
sulphuric acid was this brutal
Never did I think that this
gurgling liquid which
Reacted so well with nitric acid
to give a brown ring
Would react brutally with me

Acid burns destroyed my face
But my soul remains unscathed
What makes a woman is not her
Kohl lined eyes or mascara clad
eyelids
But her true inner self...

A woman may look sweet and
demure
But never judge her by her looks
Because she comes from the
likes of Goddess Kali
She's like mother earth
Suffering all the indignities in
silence...

Volcanoes erupt on her surface
Floods course through her
cracks and crevices
Earthquakes shake her
But she can face all these
She remains unscathed, bold as
ever...

ADVICE TO SOMEBODY'S CHILD

When somebody's child fails
others say, marks do not determine life
When somebody's child elopes
people say love is blind
When somebody's child is eliminated in an interview
people say there are thousands to come

When somebody's child tops an
exam
people blame it on the "too easy
exam"
When somebody's child marries
a good rich man
people say it won't last
When somebody's child becomes
a company head
people scan the newspapers for
a corruption scam
It's easy to advise somebody's
child easy to feel for somebody's
child

When that somebody's position
turns out for your child
How come your attitude takes
a 180 degree out of phase???...

What is love??

Is that what you and I shared when
we stared across each other in
the classroom?
Is that what set my heart racing
when you walked past
Me in the staircase?
Is that what made the blood
course through my veins?
And made me blush when you
laughed

Is that what makes me stammer
when you ask me anything?
Is it love which makes me envious
When you walk away with that
cute looking girl?
Maybe its love that holds me
back from telling you that
I love you........
Maybe it's theory of love that
stops me from telling because
love is sometimes best left as
a pain
Unsaid but still felt by each cell
of my body...

I am confused whether I am grown up or not

Woken up early morning on a bright Sunday by mom
To fetch a bag of groceries
I sulk and sink back into bed
Protesting that the shop is too far,
She counters you are a big girl, go hurry

Another bright morning
And my friends call me to

Go out for a blast of a movie
Mom sulks and says theatres
are dark and crowded
Too dangerous for little girls...

I reach college, late by let's say
five minutes
Professor swells up in fury
Shouts at the top of his lungs
It isn't play school anymore
You are too grown up act
accordingly

I chat with friends and hangout
at the college cafeteria
The same professor who
practically beheaded me in the
morning
Ushers us to go home
It's too late he says, it's dark
and you are kids after all...

I am too old for an affair
Too young for marrying!
I am too old to bunk exams
Too young to bunk classes !

I am too old to wake up late in
the morning
And too young to stay awake
late at night
I am too old to watch cartoons
Too young to be watching fashion
TV

I am too old to be taken out by
my parents
And too young to go out with my
friends
Aah the list just goes on...and on
I really wonder whether one day
I would be too old to inspire
And too young to expire